KidsGardening

A Kids' Guide to Messing Around in the Dirt

by Kevin Raftery and
Kim Gilbert Raftery

illustrated by
Jim M'Guinness

Klutz Press 🍎 Palo Alto, California

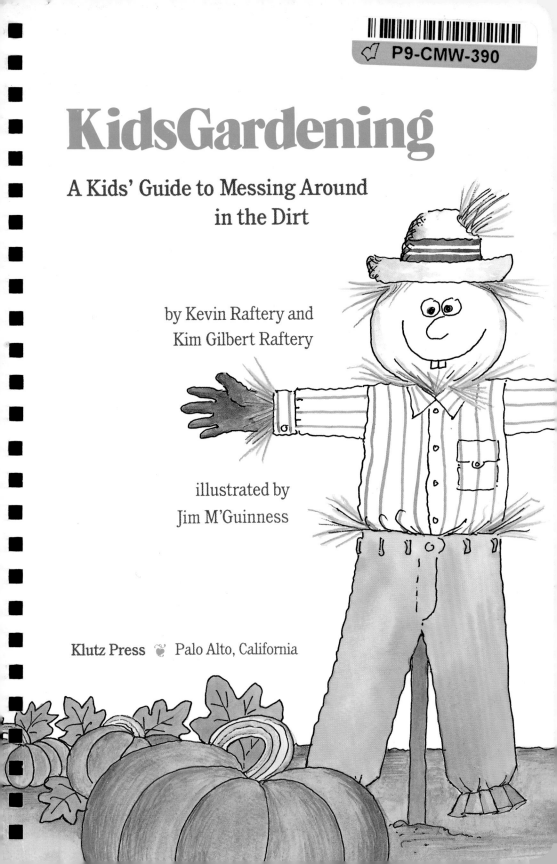

The authors would like to offer special thanks to:

All the gardeners and residents, leafy and otherwise, at the Hidden Villa Garden

The Phillips Brooks School and my second grade gardeners

John Jeavons

Craig Dremann

Design, art direction, and production: MaryEllen Podgorski and Suzanne Gooding

Illustrations: Jim M'Guinness

Editorial assistance: Anne Johnson

Lettering: Steve Kongsle

Printed in Hong Kong

Seeds produced and packed in U.S.A.

Additional copies of this book, as well as a catalogue of other Klutz books and products, are available directly from the publisher. Please address inquiries to:

Klutz Press
2121 Staunton Court
Palo Alto, CA 94306

9 8 7 6 5 4 3 2

Contents

What Plants Need to Grow

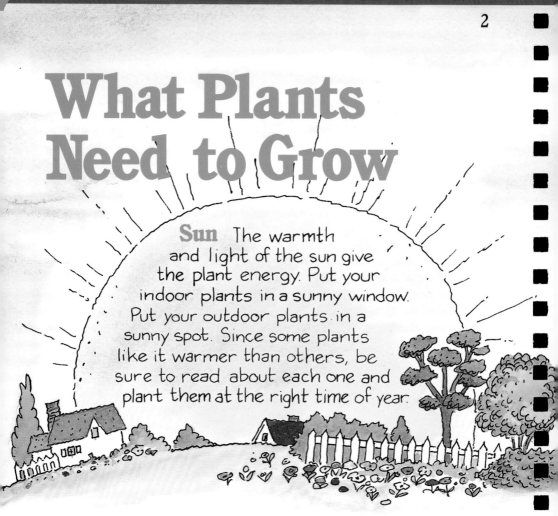

Sun The warmth and light of the sun give the plant energy. Put your indoor plants in a sunny window. Put your outdoor plants in a sunny spot. Since some plants like it warmer than others, be sure to read about each one and plant them at the right time of year.

Seeds need water to start growing, and plants need it to keep growing. Since water is so important, you have to check every day. When the soil feels dry, use a watering can or gentle sprinkler until the soil feels as damp as a wrung out sponge.

If you use too much water, the soil will get soggy or muddy--and the plant could drown. If you squirt it on too hard, the soil can wash away. Use just enough to dampen the ground--and do it carefully. Pretend you're a gentle little rainshower.

Air *Plants need air just like we do, but they breathe it through their* tops (leaves) and bottoms (roots). Their leaves can always breathe easily, but their roots have to be in loose soil. Compost or manure helps loosen the soil and let the roots breathe.

Keeping the soil loose is one of the reasons you need to be careful walking around your plants. Make a path around your garden so you don't walk on the soft soil in which your plants are breathing.

Nutrients Plant food is sometimes called "nutrients" and many of them are already in your garden soil. Preparing the soil with fertilizer or compost, and then fertilizing again later, will make your plants <u>much</u> happier.

Soil The nutrients and water go into the soil where the roots can absorb them. Healthy good soil is loosely packed and rich in air, water, nutrients and billions of microscopic plants and animals.

Getting Your Garden Ready

Before you plant your seeds or seedlings, you have to decide where your garden is going to be. It doesn't have to be a big place. Walk around with your grown-up assistant and look for a spot that gets plenty of sun, has nice soil, is close to a water faucet, and is at least 3 feet by 3 feet big.

After you've settled on a spot, you have to get started on one of the most important steps: getting the soil ready. Plain old dirt--unfertilized and unprepared--is hardly ever good enough for a really healthy garden.

You will need:

A digging fork

or

A shovel

compost

A rake

aged manure

MANURE

mulch (dry grass clippings, leaves, straw or mulch from a store)

(you can get this from a garden store)

First remove any weeds that are in your garden plot. Then with your shovel or digging fork, loosen up the soil. Dig it about a foot deep, breaking up all the hard clumps. If the dirt is too hard to dig, water it well, then come back the next day and try again.

Spread about 2 inches of compost or aged manure (see page 12 for information on where to get compost and manure) on top of your loosened soil, and mix it into the dirt with your shovel. Smooth out all the lumps and bumps with a rake and make a path around the plot so you won't step where your plants are going to be.

Plain old dirt + compost OR + mulch = SUPER-SOIL!

How to Start Seeds Growing

Turning a tiny seed into a big healthy plant is one of Mother Nature's most miraculous performances and, fortunately, she handles the tricky parts. But it is a process that you can help a great deal by using extra special care with your seeds and seedlings. Since almost every activity in this book starts from seeds, you'll need to read this part carefully.

Seeds can be started either in a container or in the ground. The steps to take are almost the same. If you decide to use containers, there's a huge variety to choose from: milk cartons, plastic buckets, cottage cheese or ice cream containers, coffee cans, paper cups, clay flower pots-- almost anything that you can make holes in the bottom of (so the water can drain) and that will hold moist soil.

Before you plant seeds, it helps to soak them overnight in water so they'll sprout more quickly. But don't do it until you're ready to plant. Once they're wet, seeds should not be allowed to dry out.

When you plant
the seeds in prepared,
fertilized soil (see pages
4+5 for information on getting your
soil ready), they have to be spaced far
enough apart and buried to the right depth.
If they're too deep, too shallow, or too close
together, they won't grow as well.

dirt   +   fertilizer   =   prepared
                                                          soil

Pat the dirt down gently after the seed is planted and water carefully. Don't make puddles or mud and don't wash the seeds away.

Don't trample...

...or flood your garden.

Every day, check the soil and water it when it feels dry on the surface. The soil should feel moist-- like a wrung-out sponge-- not soggy. Use a watering can or a gentle spray attachment on a hose.

If you planted your seeds in a container, place it in a sunny spot when the seeds sprout.

After your seeds have sprouted into seedlings, watch them as they grow. If they are too tightly grouped -- less than an inch apart -- snip off the smaller plants at the soil surface with scissors so that those that are left have enough elbow room. This is called "thinning" your plants.

You may notice that there are more seeds in the packets than you need for each activity. You can use the extra seeds to plant a larger garden if you want, or you can save them to plant next year. If you decide to save your seeds, store them in their packets in a tightly closed jar and keep the jar in a cool, dry place.

How to Feed Your Plants

Just like everybody else, plants have to have plenty of good food. Make sure your plants can put their roots into rich, healthy soil, full of plant nutrients.

What Plants Like to Eat

Plant food is called fertilizer and you can either make your own, or buy it from a store. If you go to a grocery, hardware or gardening store, the best kind to buy is either compost, aged manure or a liquid called "fish emulsion". Although plants will usually survive in unfertilized soil, they will grow <u>much much</u> better if you feed them properly with one of these fertilizers.

If you don't want to go to a store, you can make your own compost at home by keeping a compost pile. It takes some time but it's not hard; all the instructions are on page 12.

When Should You Feed Them?

Feed them on the first day, and then again every 3 or 4 weeks. If you're using liquid fish emulsion, don't put it on straight. Mix it with water, approximately one glug (one glug = 3 tablespoons) per gallon of water. If you're using aged manure or compost, just scatter a couple of handfuls around each plant and mix it into the soil.

How to Make Your Own Compost

Outdoors only.

Compost is a rich mix of weeds, leaves, kitchen scraps and grass clippings that plants love to sink their roots into. Compost is most of the difference between ordinary dirt and rich garden soil. No garden should be without it. You can buy bags of compost from a hardware or gardening store, or you can make your own. Here's the recipe.

A garden without compost...   A garden with compost...

You will need: One pile of dry things: dry leaves, dry grass clippings, dry straw or dry weeds. (Two exceptions: no Bermuda grass and no wild morning glory. These could start growing in your compost pile and spread to your garden. Ask your grown-up assistant if you have any.).

dry stuff

One pile of fresh kinds of things: kitchen scraps are great (so long as you don't include any meat, bones, or grease which will attract animals). If you have any fresh green weeds or fresh grass clippings you can put them in your compost pile too.

fresh stuff

An old, full of holes garbage can or barrel. (optional)

A shovel or digging fork

1. Find a spot (shady is better) that is near your garden and a water faucet. Incidentally, a well-kept compost pile is not like a pile of garbage. If you do it right, no smells and no flies. If yours starts smelling, it means you have used too much wet stuff or watered it too much.

2. Start your pile with a layer of dry things. Spread it out so it is about 4 inches deep and 3 feet by 3 feet.

fresh stuff
dry stuff
fresh stuff
dry stuff
fresh stuff
dry stuff
fresh stuff

Water this layer, and every other layer, to keep it damp. (If you have an old garbage can or barrel, with holes in the sides or bottom, you can put your pile in the barrel. All the instructions are the same, and it works the same-- the only difference is that it looks a little neater).

3. Then, cover your bottom layer with a similar layer of fresh or green things. Be sure to spread it out so your pile doesn't attract flies.

4. You won't really have a good compost pile until yours is about 3 feet high, but don't worry if you run out of material before that. Just cover over whatever you do have with a thin layer of dirt. Every day if you like, you can add new material. Just shovel the new material on top, cover with a little dirt and water it.

5. When you get a 3 foot tall pile, you're ready. Cover it with a little bit of soil to keep it from drying out. You might want to cover it with plastic to keep out the rain. Inside the pile, things should really start to heat up now. So hot, in fact, that you'll be cooking this material from the inside out. It takes a while, 2 to 3 months (a little sooner if you get a fork out and turn the whole thing upside down after a few weeks), but at the end of that time, your compost is ready to mix in with your garden soil.

Weeding and Mulching

Weeding

Weeds are any plants that grow where you don't want them. In your garden, weeds can crowd your plants and keep them from getting all the sun they need to grow. Make it a habit to weed your garden regularly, pulling the weeds out when they are still young.

When you plant seeds in your garden use markers to show where the rows are so you will know which plants you want to keep and which you want to pull out.

Are these guys weeds or your plants?

It can be hard to tell a weed from a plant you want to keep when they are just sprouting.

Get your grown-up assistant to help you if you aren't sure.

Mulching

Mulch is like a blanket that covers your garden and keeps weeds from growing and keeps your garden soil moist and soft.

You can use leaves, straw or grass clippings to mulch your garden or you can buy bags of it at a gardening store. If you use grass, be sure you dry it in thin layers first. One kind of grass, called "bermuda grass" isn't good for mulching. Ask if you're not sure what kind you have.

Spread the mulch 2-3 inches deep over your garden. If you are planting big seeds--like corn-- or if you're planting seedlings, you can spread the mulch right after planting. For small seeds like lettuce, don't mulch until after the seeds sprout.

Store-bought mulch

Leaves

Grass

When you're watering, be sure you use enough water to soak through the layer of mulch and into the ground.

Moving Plants

When to Move Them
Plants need elbow room to grow. If you started your seeds in a small container they will have to be moved into something larger--or into the ground--usually about a month after they have sprouted.

Frost Danger
If you're going to move your plants outdoors make sure it isn't freezing at night. One cold night of below freezing weather (less than 32°) can kill a young plant. Ask your grown-up assistant if you're not sure if this "frost danger" is over yet.

How to Move Them Outdoors

1. When your plants are ready to move, make sure there's no chance of frost, then take them outside. Leave them in their containers for a few days so they can get used to the idea of the great outdoors.

2. While you're waiting, decide where you want your plants to go and prepare the soil (see instructions on page 4). Once your plants are accustomed to being outdoors, and once you've prepared the soil, you can make the move. Wait until the cooler part of the day and then dig a small hole. Water the soil until it is moist, but not soaking or muddy.

3. Carefully dig up the roots of your plants with your hand or little shovel. Try to keep as much dirt around the roots as possible.

4. Put the roots and lower stem into the hole and cover them with soil up to about the lowest leaves. If your hole wasn't big enough, make it bigger now --don't scrunch the roots.

5. Water well so that the loosened soil will settle around the roots of the seedling.

6. Put about two inches of mulch, straw or grass cuttings around the new plant to discourage weeds and to keep the dirt moist.

Garden Pests and Friends

There are few insects that really deserve to be called bugs. These pests will sometimes eat the weak or young plants in your garden. They tend to leave the healthy plants alone, so the best thing you can do is keep your plants strong by giving them good soil, and all the fertilizer, water, and sun that they need.

If you see holes chewed in the leaves of your plants, or your seedlings are disappearing mysteriously, you've probably got hungry caterpillars, slugs or snails in your garden. Check your garden early in the morning and collect any of the pests you find. Look on the undersides of leaves, under flower pots or any dark place where they might be hiding.

Slugs and snails are especially fond of
midnight snacks, so the best time
to find them is after dark.
Take a flashlight out with
you and put all the slugs
and snails you find
in a jar. If you
know any
chickens,
you
can
give
your
collection
to them for a treat. If you don't know any chickens, take
the slugs and snails out to an open field where they can't
do any damage to gardens.

A lot of bugs that like to lunch in your
garden are too small to pick off by hand. You can
send these on their way with a strong spray of
water from a hose. Bugs hate the taste of soap,
so if you spray them with a little soapy water,
you can get rid of them without hurting your
plants.

But remember that not all bugs are bad. There
are a lot of bugs that are good for your garden too.
Bees and butterflies pollinate your flowers, worms
turn dead leaves into fertilizer, and lady bugs and other
insects love to eat the bugs that love to eat your
garden. Birds, snakes, lizards, and frogs also help
by eating garden pests.

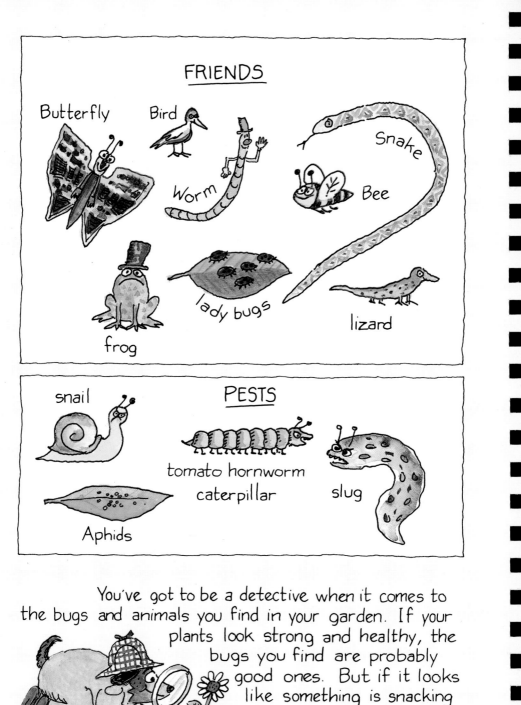

FRIENDS

Butterfly

Bird

Worm

Snake

Bee

lady bugs

lizard

frog

PESTS

snail

tomato hornworm
caterpillar

slug

Aphids

You've got to be a detective when it comes to the bugs and animals you find in your garden. If your plants look strong and healthy, the bugs you find are probably good ones. But if it looks like something is snacking on your leaves or seedlings, you need to find the bad guys and do what you can to get rid of them.

Bug Bottle

You will need:

A cooperative caterpillar, beetle, grasshopper, snail, slug or spider

Some leaves

A little moist dirt

A large jar with holes punched in the lid (get your grown up assistant to help)

Put a little moist soil in the bottom of your jar.

Walk through your garden and see if you can find any interesting bugs, slugs or snails. Stay away from wasps, bees, and black widow spiders.

When you find something good, gently move it into your jar. It's a good idea to put a few leaves or a little twig in the jar so your bug feels at home.

Your bug will need a little something to eat. Snails, slugs, grasshoppers and caterpillars like to eat leaves, especially lettuce. Ladybugs eat aphids. Praying mantises and spiders like flies.

Keep your jar indoors out of the sun and heat. Every day or two, add a few drops of water and maybe a fresh leaf. Check your bug often to see what it's up to.

After a week, return your bug to your garden (or if you had a slug or snail, to an open field) and find another one.

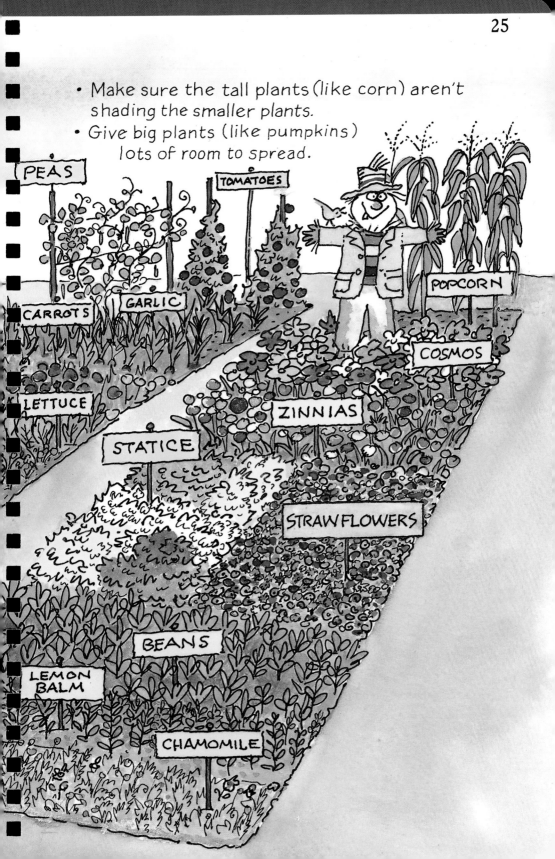

Lettuce

Start in spring or fall.

Grow indoors or outdoors, in containers or in the ground.

You will need:

12 lettuce seeds

FISH-O Liquid fertilizer

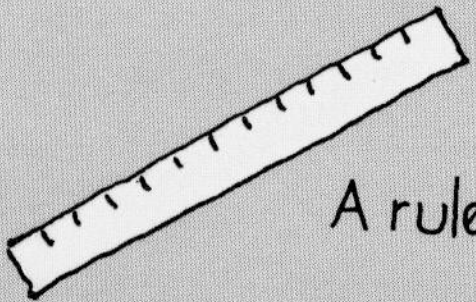

A ruler

container of prepared soil, at least 3 inches deep

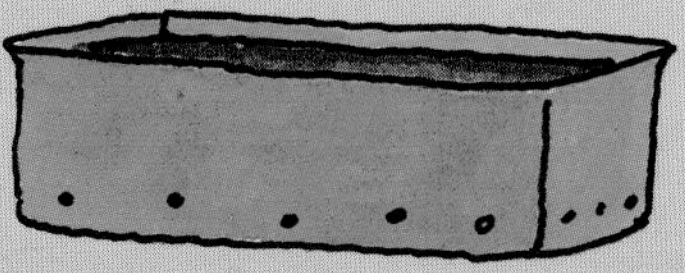

A 3 ft. × 3 ft. garden spot of prepared soil **OR** several half-gallon containers filled with soil

← 8" →

MILK

1. Fill your container with prepared soil (see page 4 for instructions on how to prepare soil).

2. Plant your lettuce seeds 2 inches apart and ⅛ inch deep (only this deep ↕).   Be careful, seeds that are buried too deeply wont sprout. Water gently.

3. Place the container in a sunny spot and water gently every time the soil dries out. In about 10 days, the seeds will sprout.

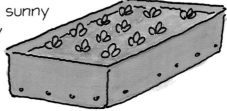

4. When the seedlings get to be 2 inches tall, they'll have to be moved. You can move them into the ground, or into 12 individual containers, each of them about the size of a cut-off half-gallon milk carton.

MULCH

5. If you're moving into the ground, prepare a 3 foot by 3 foot spot in your garden. Plant your seedlings in 3 rows and space them carefully. When you're done, water everybody well and mulch with grass cuttings, straw or leaves to keep the weeds down.

6. If you're moving into larger containers, make sure they're all big enough, then fill them with fertilized soil, dig a hole big enough for the roots, and carefully move your seedlings into their new homes. Water gently, move them into sunny windows, and check every day so the soil doesn't dry out.

7. Feed your plants with dilute liquid fertilizer every 3-4 weeks.

8. In 6 to 8 weeks, the lettuce leaves will be ready to pick. You can pick the outside leaves individually and let more grow, or you can harvest the whole head.

Radishes

Grow anytime.

Grow indoors or outdoors, in the ground, or in a container.

Radishes are going to be your garden's fast food, the quickest growing vegetable in this book. Figure one month from start to stomach. And incidentally, you only <u>think</u> you don't like radishes. Grow them yourself and they'll taste as good as sugar plums. Well, almost as good.

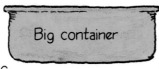

32 radish seeds

A ruler

Big container

Several containers filled with fertilized soil, at least 6 inches deep **or** a garden spot about 2 feet by 2 feet

1. Plant your seeds (indoors or out, in a container or not, it doesn't matter) about 3 inches apart and ⅛ inch deep. Make sure your soil is prepared and ready for your seeds. See page 4 for instructions. Water them gently. Indoor gardeners, be sure to put them in a sunny window.

2. Check the soil surface every day and keep it moist -- like a wrung-out sponge. In about a week your seeds should be sprouting. Now is a good time to mulch around the seedlings. Use grass cuttings, straw, or leaves.

3. In 3 to 4 weeks, your radishes should be ready to harvest. Pick the biggest ones first and cut them into a salad, or just eat them right out of the garden. (Really! Try it.)

Carrots

Start in spring.
Grow outdoors in containers or in the ground.

Pulling a sweet, home-grown carrot out of your garden is like finding a buried treasure in your own backyard.

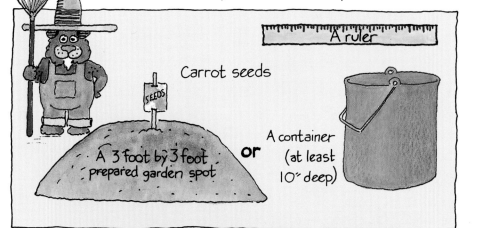

A ruler

Carrot seeds

A 3 foot by 3 foot prepared garden spot

or

A container (at least 10" deep)

1. First, soak your carrot seeds overnight in water the day before you want to plant them.

2. The next step is to get your garden ready. (This is an important step. Don't skip it!) See page 4 for the instructions. Since carrots grow straight down, prepare the dirt deeply, 12 inches or so.

If you're using a container, fill it with prepared dirt. Remember to fertilize.

3. After you're done preparing the dirt, pour the water off your seeds and spread them out to dry on a paper towel for no more than 15 minutes. Keep them out of direct sunlight.

If you are planting in the ground...

1. Make 3 rows in the soil ⅛ of an inch deep (this deep ↕) and 8 inches apart. If your seeds are too deep or not deep enough, they might not grow. Put the seeds in the rows about an inch apart, then pat the soil over them so they end up ⅛ of an inch underground.

Put seed here, ⅛" deep...

...then cover them over.

If you are using containers...

1. Spread your seeds out across the dirt so that they are at least an inch apart. Sprinkle an ⅛ inch layer of dirt over them, and pat it down.

2. Water very gently so you don't wash the tiny seeds away. Mulch the soil lightly with a fine compost to keep it moist.

3. Carrot seeds will not sprout if they get even a little bit dry, but on the other hand, they don't like it if they get drowned in a flood. Keep the dirt moist, so it feels like a wrung-out sponge. Check it every day. You can cover the soil with burlap or an old sheet until the seeds sprout to keep the soil moist.

No matter where you're planting...

1. In about 2 to 3 weeks, the seeds will sprout. When the carrots are young, they'll need only an inch between them, but as they get bigger, they'll need more room. After a month or so, pick enough of the small carrots so that those that are left have 4 inches between them. Incidentally, the tiny carrots are great eating! Don't throw them away.

Thinning your carrots.

2. Check every day and water before the soil dries out. Every 3 to 4 weeks sprinkle with a gallon of dilute liquid fertilizer. In about 3 to 4 months your carrots should be full grown. To make sure, clear away the dirt from the base of the leaves. Your carrot is ready to pull if you can see its top.

Tomatoes

Start in early spring, a month or so before last frost.

Start indoors; finish outdoors in containers or the ground.

Cherry tomatoes are small in size but BIG in flavor. They're sweet and easy to eat. Just pick them off the vine, and pop them into your mouth.

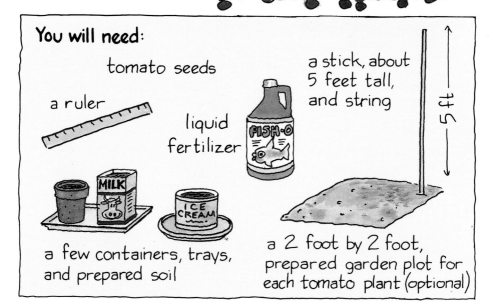

You will need:

tomato seeds

a ruler

liquid fertilizer

a stick, about 5 feet tall, and string

5 ft

a few containers, trays, and prepared soil

a 2 foot by 2 foot, prepared garden plot for each tomato plant (optional)

1. Tomatoes should be started in containers, indoors. For each plant that you want to grow, start with 3 tomato seeds and a container that is at least 6 inches deep and 4 inches wide.

2. Fill each container with fertilized soil, then in each of them, plant 3 seeds about 1 inch apart and ⅛ of an inch deep. Water gently.

3. Every day, check the soil and keep it moist.

4. After about two weeks, when your seedlings appear, move the containers to a sunny window and keep watering regularly. When the seedlings are about 4 inches high, leave the healthiest looking plant in each container and use a pair of scissors to snip off the other two.

5. When danger of frost has passed and the seedlings are at least 6 inches high, you can move them outdoors into larger containers, or into the ground. See page 18 for how to move plants.

6. If you are going to raise your plants in containers, they will have to be at least a foot deep. Fill them with fertilized soil, dig out holes big enough for the roots and lower stem, and place your carefully uprooted plants in them. Re-fill the holes so that the lower leaves are at the surface of the soil. Water well and put everybody in very sunny spots.

7. If you are going to raise your plants in the ground you'll need to get a 2 foot by 2 foot garden spot ready for each seedling. Move your plants into big enough holes, refill to the lowest leaves, then water well and mulch the soil.

8. When your plants are about 1 foot tall, carefully place a stick in the ground right next to the stem and loosely tie the two together for support.

9. Check the dirt every day and keep it moist. Try not to get the tomato leaves wet. Water the plants with dilute liquid fertilizer every 3-4 weeks.

10. 2 or 3 months after you transplant the seedlings, the tomatoes will be ready to harvest.

Kim's Ranch Dressing

Every year, Kim polls her 2nd grade class on their favorite salad dressing. And every year the answer is the same: Ranch Style. See below for the official 2nd grade approved recipe.

1. Mix all the following in a small bowl and stir well:

- ½ cup mayonnaise
- ½ cup buttermilk (or plain yogurt)
- ¼ teaspoon salt
- 1 small clove crushed garlic (OR ¼ teaspoon garlic powder)
- ½ teaspoon onion powder
- 1 teaspoon dried parsley powder

Pumpkins

Start in spring after frost danger is passed.
Grow outdoors in ground.

Growing carrots and other leafy things is fine, but it's not until you get a real 10 pound orange monster growing that you know you're really GARDENING!

You will need:

3 pumpkin seeds

liquid fertilizer

FISHO

A ruler

A 3 foot by 3 foot prepared garden spot

1. As usual, the first step is very important: prepare the spot you're going to plant in. Pages 4-5 have all the instructions. (Incidentally, aged manure from the garden store is a favorite of pumpkins.)

2. Plant your seeds in the middle of your spot 8 inches apart and about 1 inch deep.

3. Water the soil and mulch it with grass cuttings, leaves, straw, or store bought mulch.

4. Every day, check the dirt to make sure it hasn't gotten too dry. Water it so that it feels moist (but not soggy).

5. After about 10 days, the seeds will sprout. Wait a few weeks and pull the smallest of the three plants and put it in the compost pile if you have one.

6. Pumpkins are big eaters and drinkers. Use a gallon of your diluted liquid fertilizer mix once every 3-4 weeks and keep the soil moist.

7. In 3 to 4 months, your pumpkins will be ready to harvest. Pick them before the first frost when they're bright orange. If you leave about 3 inches of stem, your pumpkins will keep much better.

Personalized Pumpkin

Use a ball point pen and write your name on your pumpkin when it is still small. Break the skin a little and as your pumpkin grows, so will your name.

Roasted Pumpkin Seeds

Eat anytime; especially good around Halloween.

Whenever you cut a pumpkin open to make a jack-o-lantern, save the seeds and try this recipe. Roasted pumpkin seeds make great munchies.

pumpkin seeds from one pumpkin

A bowl

2 Tbls. vegetable oil.

A cookie sheet

A couple of paper towels

A little salt

1. Cut your pumpkin open and scoop out all the seeds. Rinse them with water to remove all the stringy stuff. Spread the seeds out on paper towels for a few hours to dry.

2. Once the seeds are dry, preheat your oven to 250°

3. Put the seeds in the bowl and add the oil and a little salt. Mix it all together.

4. Spread the seeds on a cookie sheet and bake for about an hour. Stir the seeds around every fifteen minutes.

5. Let your seeds cool a little bit before you start eating them.

Cucumbers

Start in spring.
Grow outdoors in containers or in the ground.

3 cucumber seeds

liquid
fertilizer

A
ruler

One large container
(3-5 gallon) **or**

A 3×3 foot
garden
plot

SEEDS

1. Prepare your garden plot, or if you are using a container, fill it with prepared soil.

2. Plant three seeds in the middle of your garden plot or container. The seeds should be about two inches apart and one inch deep.

3. Water and mulch the soil.

4. Check your garden every day and water to keep soil moist.

5. Your cucumbers will sprout in about 10 days. In two more weeks, once the plants have grown a few leaves, you'll have to thin them. If your cucumbers are growing in the ground, pull out one of the cucumber plants and leave the strongest two still growing. If you're using a container, pull out two seedlings and leave the biggest growing.

6. Cucumbers like a lot of water and fertilizer. Keep the dirt moist, and feed them dilute liquid fertilizer once a month. Try to keep the leaves dry so they don't mildew.

Dilute liquid fertilizer = 3 tablespoons liquid fertilizer + 1 gal. H_2O

7. You can start harvesting your cucumbers after two or three months. Pick them when they are about 8 inches long and 2-3 inches thick. Don't wait too long to pick your cucumbers or they will turn yellow and taste bitter.

Fresh Pickles

You can put your cucumbers to good use by making your own pickles. These pickles only last two weeks, but they'll probably get eaten in the first week anyway.

2 empty jars

1 tablespoon dill

1 tablespoon salt

1 teaspoon mustard seed

3 medium sized cucumbers

1 cup vinegar

1 clove garlic

2 cups water

6 whole black peppercorns

1. Wash the cucumbers and cut each one in half, crosswise. Cut each half lengthwise into four pieces. You might want to ask your grown-up assistant for help with this part.

2. Put the cut cucumbers in a large bowl and sprinkle the salt and dill over them. Use your hands to mix them so they are all evenly coated.

3. Let the cucumbers sit for half an hour.

4. Put the cucumbers into two jars. Add three peppercorns and ½ tsp. mustard seed to each jar (you'll find both in the spice section of your grocery store).

5. Peel the garlic clove and cut it in half. Using a garlic press, squeeze one half into each jar.

6. Stir the water and vinegar together in a large measuring cup or bowl. Pour half into each jar.

7. Screw the lids on tightly. Shake each jar to be sure everything is well mixed.

8. Put the pickles in the refrigerator. Wait until the next day to eat them.

9. Your pickles will last up to two weeks in the refrigerator.

Sugar Snap Peas

Spring or fall.
Grow in containers or in the ground.

These pea pods taste so good just off the vine that they may never make it to the dinner table.

One five foot pole or stick for each container (or three poles if you are planting in the ground)

2-10 pea seeds (use 10 if you're planting in the ground)

liquid fertilizer

FISH-O

One five gallon container for every two seeds

OR:

A 1 x 5 foot garden plot

GREAT BIG PICKLES

A ruler

A ball of string (If you are planting in the ground)

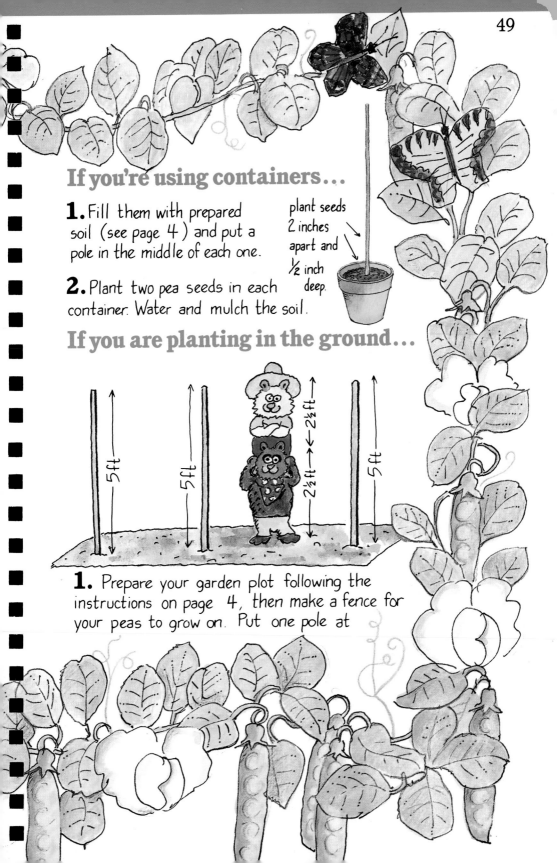

If you're using containers...

1. Fill them with prepared soil (see page 4) and put a pole in the middle of each one.

plant seeds 2 inches apart and ½ inch deep.

2. Plant two pea seeds in each container. Water and mulch the soil.

If you are planting in the ground...

5ft   5ft   2½ft ←→ 2½ft   5ft

1. Prepare your garden plot following the instructions on page 4, then make a fence for your peas to grow on. Put one pole at

wrap tightly around each pole.

PEAS

each end of your plot and one in the middle. Tie the end of the string to the top of one of the end poles. Run the string to the middle pole, wrap it around once, then move on the last pole. Wrap the string around this pole once, then go back to the middle pole. Work back and forth like this, wrapping the string a couple of inches closer to the ground each time you turn around.

2. Plant 10 pea seeds six inches apart and a half an inch deep just under the fence. Water and mulch the soil.

Wherever you're growing…

3. The seeds will sprout in a couple of weeks. Be sure the vines are growing up the poles or the fence you've made. You may have to help them until they get started.

4. Water the plants with dilute liquid fertilizer every 3 – 4 weeks.

5. In about two or three months the plants will start to make flowers. Don't pick them, because they will grow into pea pods. When these are about two inches long, you can pick them or cut them off with scissors. You can cook them for dinner, but they really do taste best right there in the garden.

Beans

Grow outdoors in spring or summer.
Plant in containers or in the ground.

The dried beans in your cupboard are really bean seeds. You can plant these beans to grow new bean plants. Try growing a mix and see what you come out with.

A ruler

12 dry beans
(any kind but split peas will work)

A 3 by 3 foot plot of ground or 6 medium sized containers

FISH-O liquid fertilizer

3 ft.

If you're planting in the ground...

1. Prepare your garden soil and make two rows 12 inches apart.

2. Plant 6 beans in a row, keeping the seeds 6 inches apart and ½" deep.

If you're planting in containers...

1. Fill your containers with prepared soil.

2. Plant 2 seeds in each container, ½ inch deep, keeping the seeds at least 3 inches apart.

Wherever you're planting...

1. Water enough to keep the soil moist, and feed with liquid fertilizer about once a month.

2. The seeds will sprout in a couple of weeks. If you planted in the ground pull out every other bean so the plants are 12 inches away from each other. Leave one bean growing in each container. Mulch the soil.

3. After 2 or 3 months your bean plants will flower, and little bean pods will start to grow. Leave the beans on the vine until the pods dry out.

4. When the pods are dry, you can harvest them. Crumble the bean pods in your hands and the beans will drop right out. When you're sure they're good and dry, store the beans in a jar or a plastic bag until you want to eat them (they're great in vegetable soup).

Fresh Flower Bouquets

Fresh flower bouquets of cosmos, marigolds, and zinnias.
Start in spring outdoors in containers or ground.

flower seeds
(8 each of cosmos, marigolds, and zinnias)

A ruler

6 big pots
(at least 12 inches deep)

or

A
3×6 foot
garden plot

liquid
fertilizer

If you are using containers...

1. Fill each pot with prepared dirt.

2. Plant 4 seeds of one kind of flower in each pot. Leave at least 2 inches between each seed, and cover them all with about ⅛ of an inch of soil.

3. Be sure to mark each pot with the name of the flower you planted in it, then give them all some water.

If you are planting in the ground...

1. Get your garden ready (see pages 4+5) and make two long rows running the length of the plot. Now divide your plot into three even sections.

2. Each flower gets its own section. When you plant the seeds, keep them at least 6 inches apart and cover them with ⅛ of an inch of dirt.

3. Water everything and make a sign for each section naming the flower growing there.

4. Check the soil every day and keep it moist.

5. The seeds will sprout in about 2 weeks. When they do, it's time to mulch the soil.

Pull these

6. When the seedlings are about 3 inches tall, you'll have to thin them. Pull out all but one seedling from each container or all but 4 from each garden section. Try to leave the biggest strongest looking plants growing.

7. Water with dilute liquid fertilizer every 3-4 weeks.

8. When you water the plants, try to keep the leaves dry and just water the ground they are standing in.

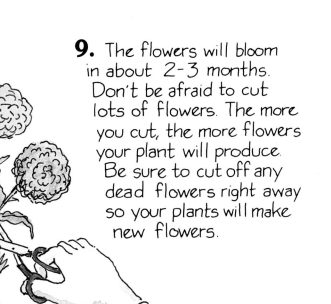

9. The flowers will bloom in about 2-3 months. Don't be afraid to cut lots of flowers. The more you cut, the more flowers your plant will produce. Be sure to cut off any dead flowers right away so your plants will make new flowers.

Everlasting Flowers

Start in spring.

Grow outdoors in pots or in the ground.

These flowers can be gathered and made into fresh bouquets, or dried and made into bouquets that will last a very long time.

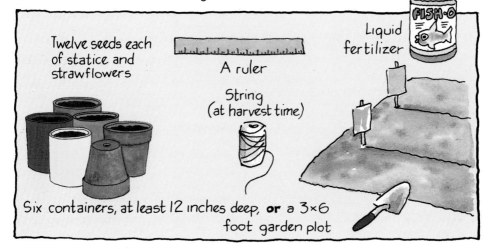

Twelve seeds each of statice and strawflowers

A ruler

String (at harvest time)

Liquid fertilizer

FISH-O

Six containers, at least 12 inches deep, **or** a 3×6 foot garden plot

The statice and strawflower seeds are mixed together in the packet. Carefully pour the seeds onto a plate and sort them into two piles. The statice seeds are smaller and darker than the strawflower seeds.

If you're using containers...

MILK

straw flowers

1. Fill the pots with fertilized soil.

2. Plant each kind of flower in its own container. Plant four seeds in each one, keeping them 2 inches apart.

Cover them with ⅛ inch of soil. Remember to label each pot and water the seeds.

If you're planting in the ground...

1. Prepare your garden plot and split it into two sections, one for statice and one for strawflowers. Make two long rows in each half.

2. Plant the seeds in the rows you just made, keeping the seeds 2 inches apart. Cover them with ⅛ inch of dirt and give them some water.

Wherever you're planting...

1. Check your garden or pots every day to be sure the soil is still moist.

2. The seeds will sprout in about two weeks. When they do, you should mulch the soil.

3. When the seedlings are about three inches tall, you will have to pull some out. Leave one seedling in each pot, or six seedlings in each

Pull these to thin your plants

↑ ↑ ↑   ↑ ↑ ↑ ↑

|←—12"—→|

half of your garden. There should be about 12 inches between each plant now. Fertilize every 3-4 weeks. Keep the leaves and flowers dry by watering close to the ground.

How to Make a Dried Flower Bouquet

A flower bouquet is a beautiful present, just make sure whoever you give it to knows you grew it yourself.

1. Your flowers won't all bloom at the same time, but after about three months, you should see the first blossoms. If you harvest them as they bloom, it will be many weeks before you'll have them all collected.

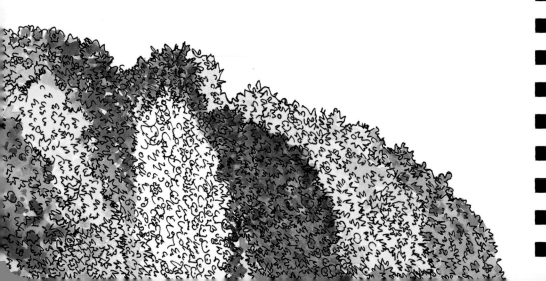

2. When you have a good bunch of flowers blooming, you can cut them off (leave about 8 inches of stem on each flower). Harvest the strawflowers before they have fully opened. Tie the bunch together with string and hang it upside down in a dry shady place. In about three weeks your flowers will be ready. Since they're dried, there's no need to put water in the vase with them.

Herbs

Lemon Balm, Chamomile and Oregano

Outdoors, start in
spring/summer.

Indoors, anytime.

Grow in containers or
in the ground.

Herbs are plants
with a little bit of magic in
them. Some have a strong
flavor and are used in
cooking, some have
such a powerful
aroma they are
kept for their smell alone, still others are used as medicine.
The three plants in this activity, lemon balm, chamomile
and oregano are all herbs. Lemon balm and chamomile have
a pleasant taste and fragrance. They can be made into
tea or bound in sweet-smelling bags called sachets. Oregano
is a powerful spice used in the kitchen, especially in italian
cooking.

Herb seeds
(12 of each kind)

A ruler

MILK

COFF

six containers
or
a 3 foot
by 3 foot
garden
spot
of prepared
soil

FISH-O

Liquid
fertilizer

String
(for harvest time)

If you are using containers...

1. Pick containers that are at least as big as a half-gallon milk carton. Fill each of them with prepared soil (see page 4 for instructions on preparing soil).

plant here, one inch apart

2. Give each herb its own container. Be sure to make labels so you can tell them apart. Plant 6 seeds in each container, keeping them 1 inch apart and cover with ⅛ of an inch of dirt.

plant your seeds only an ⅛ of an inch deep

If you are planting in the ground...

1. Make sure your garden soil has been prepared. Divide your garden into three sections, all the same size.

2. Make one long row in each section. Each herb gets its own section. Don't forget to make a sign for each section. Now plant the seeds in their rows. The seeds should be 3 inches apart and covered with an ⅛ of an inch of dirt.

Don't forget to:

Loosen...   mulch   and water

Wherever you're planting...

1. Check your garden or pots every day. Water if the dirt starts to dry out.

2. Your herbs will sprout in about 2-3 weeks. Mulch the soil now. When the seedlings are about two inches tall, you'll need to pull some of them out. Leave one seedling in each pot or 3 in each section of your garden (they'll need about a foot of space between them). Water with dilute liquid fertilizer every 3-4 weeks.

Pull two

3. In about 2 months, the lemon balm and oregano will be ready to harvest. If you cut the stem off about 2 inches above the ground, your plant will grow back and you will have more to harvest in a few weeks.

4. You'll have to wait an extra month or so for the chamomile to be ready, because it takes longer to make flowers. When you harvest the flowers, cut them with stems about 6 inches long. Don't cut the chamomile as close to the ground as you did the other herbs.

5. You can use the herbs fresh, but you'll probably want to dry them. To do this, tie a string around the cut stems, and hang them upside-down in a dry place for 3-4 weeks.

6. When the herbs are completely dry they are ready to be stored. Pull the oregano and lemon balm leaves off of the stems and cut the chamomile flowers off of their stems. You won't be using the stems, so put them in your compost pile. Put each herb in its own jar or plastic bag and label.

How to use your herbs...

1. You can use the lemon balm and chamomile to make your own tea. Use one teaspoon of each herb for each cup of tea you want. If you like your tea hot, brew it in boiling water. You can make sun tea by putting the herbs and some cold water in a big jar. Set the jar outside in a sunny spot for a couple of hours. When it's ready, pour it over ice and add some honey or sugar if you want.

2. The lemon balm and chamomile will make sweet smelling sachets too. Crumble a handful of each herb into little pieces. Pile the crumbled herbs into the middle of a handkerchief or bandana. Bring the corners of the handkerchief together and tie it with a ribbon. If you like to sew, you can make a little bag for your sachet, fill it with the herbs and tie it with a ribbon. Put your sachet anywhere you'd like to find a sweet smell, in your closet or drawers or next to your pillow.

3. The oregano is good cooked in soup, spaghetti sauce or any Italian food.

Kitchen Gardening

Grow anytime.

You can turn your kitchen into an indoor jungle any time of the year. Avocados and sweet potatoes love to grow in water-filled jars and will make your kitchen seem just a little wilder.

Avocado

One avocado pit

A glass jar

Three toothpicks

A large container filled with fertilized soil

1. The next time you get the chance, save an avocado pit. Let it dry out for a day or two, then carefully remove the brown skin. Stick in the toothpicks around the middle of the pit.

2. Fill the jar with water and put the avocado pit in with the pointy end up. The bottom

should be resting in the water. Add more if it's not. Keep the jar in a room that gets plenty of sun, but don't put it in direct sunlight. Every few days replace the water.

3. Within a few weeks the seed will start to split and you'll see a root coming out of the bottom. When this happens, it's time to plant your tree-to-be in a container. Plant it right in the middle so it's covered with an inch of

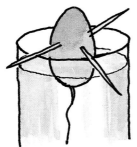

dirt. Give it some water and place it in a sunny spot. Remember that your tree will grow towards the sun, so if you want it to grow up straight you'll have to turn the pot every week or so.

4. Water regularly and fertilize every 3-4 weeks. With luck, your plant will grow into an avocado tree that will last for a long time.

Sweet Potato

You will need:

A sweet potato

A glass jar

Three toothpicks

1. Stick the three toothpicks in around the middle of the sweet potato like you did for the avocado pit.

2. Fill the jar with water and put the potato on top. It doesn't matter which end is in the jar, but be sure that the potato is resting in the water. Put the jar in a light but not too sunny place and change the water every few days.

3. In about a week the potato will sprout and start growing leaves. Your sweet potato vine will last for several months as long as you remember to give it fresh water every few days.

Guacamole

If you make this recipe often, you'll always have a fresh supply of avocado seeds. You will need:

1 green onion

3 ripe avocados

1 clove garlic

a garlic press

1 tomato

2 tbls. of mexican salsa (if you like your guacamole spicy)

1 tbls. lemon juice

1. Cut each avocado in half and dig out the pits with a spoon. Set them aside so you can start your own avocado tree. Scoop the insides into a bowl and mash them all up with a fork.

2. Wash the green onion and tomato, then chop them up and add them to the bowl.

3. Peel the garlic clove (you might want to ask for help with this part) and squeeze it through a garlic press into the mashed up avocado.

4. Add the lemon juice and the salsa (if you're using it) and stir it all together.

5. Eat the guacamole with your favorite corn chips.

Pineapple

Start anytime indoors.

Pineapples grow in warm, sunny places around the world. But even if you don't live on a tropical island you can grow your own pineapple plant.

You will need:

A pineapple

A ½ gallon milk carton cut in half

A big container or flower pot

A sharp knife and a grown up assistant

A plate

clean sand (not from the ocean)

potting soil

1. At the grocery store, pick out a ripe pineapple with a big, green, healthy looking top.

2. Cut the top of the pineapple off, leaving about an inch of fruit. You'll probably need a grown-up helper for this because pineapples are hard to cut. Save the fruit for breakfast.

3. Lay the pineapple top on its side on the plate and let it sit for two days to dry out.

4. Fill the milk carton with sand. Be sure the container has holes in the bottom so water can drain out.

5. Push the pineapple into the sand so the bottom is just covered and the leaves are pointing up. Keep the container indoors in a sunny, warm spot.

6. Water the plant enough to keep the sand moist. Every day or two, pour a little water right onto the leaves. They should be green and prickly.

7. Check for roots after about two months. When you find them, move your plant to the big container. Cover the roots with potting soil, so just the green leaves show.

8. Water with dilute liquid fertilizer every month or so.

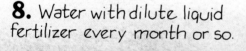

Dilute liquid fertilizer = 3 tablespoons liquid fertilizer + 1 gal. H_2O

9. If you're lucky, your plant will produce a flower stalk with a pineapple at the top (this takes a long time). But even if you never do get a pineapple on your plant, you'll have a beautiful tropical plant.

Growing a Fruit Tree

Start anytime indoors.

Transplant outdoors in spring or fall.

Trees are the granddaddies of plants. They grow to be very old, they get to be very big and they don't grow very fast. A single tree can be a friend for a lifetime, so be careful with the seed and be careful when the tree is very young. Fruit trees won't have any fruit for you to eat for a few years, so you'll have to be patient. When it finally comes, it might not be exactly like the fruit it came from, but it will taste very special because you grew it yourself.

You will need:

five fruit seeds

Liquid fertilizer

A big container

1. The first thing you have to do is decide what kind of tree you want to grow. Lemon, orange, plum, apple-- pick your favorite and save five seeds the next time you get a chance (they aren't with this book).

2. Some fruit seeds will only sprout after winter. You can fool them into thinking it's winter by putting them in the refrigerator for awhile. Orange seeds can be planted right away, but plum and apple seeds should be stored in the refrigerator in a plastic bag with a little moist soil for 3-4 months before you plant them.

3. Once the seeds are ready to plant, put them all in a large container 3 inches apart. Cover with a ½ inch of prepared soil,

plant here in prepared soil 3 inches apart
↓ ↓ ↓ ↓ ↓

and water them so that the dirt stays moist. (Note: Plum seeds have to be planted 1 inch deep.)

save this one and...

...pull the others.

4. The seeds will sprout in a few weeks. When the seedlings are two inches tall, you'll have to pull some of them out. Leave the strongest looking plant, and pull the others out. Put the pot near a sunny window. Your tree will grow towards the sun, so remember to turn the container every week to keep it growing straight.

5. Your tree can live indoors for many years. Fertilize it about once a month with dilute liquid fertilizer. If it gets too big, you can trim the branches or move it outdoors into the ground.

½ cup

Mix the liquid fertilizer with water before you use it.

6. If you decide to move your tree outdoors, wait until spring or fall. Find a sunny spot and dig a hole twice as long as the container it is already growing in. Mix some compost in with the dirt from the hole (1 part compost to 4 parts dirt). Put your tree in the hole and fill it up with dirt. Water very well. It helps to make a shallow well around your tree to hold water.

7. Feed your tree fertilizer every spring and summer.

Popcorn

Start in spring after frost danger is passed.
Grow outdoors in ground.

You can grow corn plants from the popcorn in your cupboard. It may taste a little different from the popcorn you're used to, but who knows, yours may be even better than what you started with.

20 popcorn seeds (they're in your kitchen)

HERMAN MELVILLE'S POPCORN

A 3×6 foot garden plot

Liquid fertilizer

FISH-O

A ruler

1. First, prepare your garden soil and make 2 rows 18 inches apart down the length of it. Don't plant your popcorn near any sweet corn.

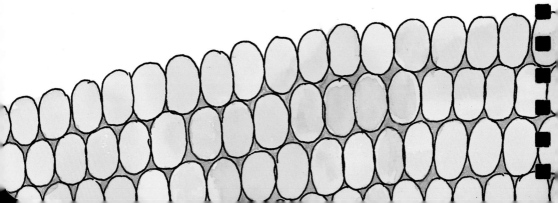

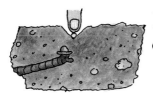

2. Plant 10 seeds in each row, ¼ inch deep and 6 inches apart.

3. Water the seeds well, then mulch the soil.

4. After 2 weeks the seeds will sprout. Thin the seedlings so that there are 12 inches between each one. Fertilize with dilute liquid fertilizer once a month.

5. After about 3 months, you should start to see ears of corn appear. In 4 months your popcorn should be ready to harvest. Leave the ears of corn on the plant to dry or cut them off the plant, peel the husks back and let them dry in a warm room for 2 to 3 weeks.

6. When the corn kernels are completely dry, you can remove them from the cob. Spread a newspaper out on a table to catch the loose kernels. Grab one ear of corn with both hands and hold over the newspaper. Twist one hand away from your body and the other towards your body (like you would wring out a towel). Move your hands back and forth like this until the kernels have all come off. Then take them into the kitchen and get popping!

Harvest after 4 months...

Peel the husks back...

Let them dry for 2 to 3 weeks

Garlic Braids

Grow in containers or in the ground. In cold areas, start in spring.

Everywhere else, in late summer. You can grow garlic indoors anytime.

A ruler

liquid fertilizer

One big, fresh bulb of garlic from the grocery store

A 2x2 foot plot **OR** A couple of big containers

1. Prepare the garden plot, or if you're using containers, fill them with prepared dirt.

ROCKY'S ROADSIDE VEGGIES

2. Break the garlic into individual cloves. Be sure to leave the papery skin on each one. Now pick out the twelve biggest cloves. Be sure none of them are rotten (rotten cloves would be soft and squishy).

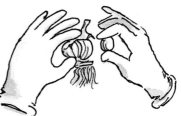

3. If you are planting outdoors, make three evenly spaced rows in your garden plot.

4. Whether you're growing your garlic in a container or in the ground, plant the cloves 5 inches apart. The pointy end of the clove is the top. Push each clove into the ground so that the top is covered by about 2 inches of soil. Pat the soil down, give the garlic some water, and mulch it.

correct planting of cloves, pointy end up

2"

5"

5. Your garlic will sprout in just a few weeks. Be careful that the soil doesn't dry out.

6. Water the plants once a month with liquid fertilizer while it's still warm outside. You can stop when it gets cold.

7. After about 5 months, the garlic leaves will turn yellow. When this happens, stop watering them.

GARLIC FOR SALE CHEAP

FIDO

8. When the leaves are completely yellow, it's time to harvest. It is important to harvest your garlic before the leaves get dry and crunchy, or you wont be able to braid it.

9. To harvest your garlic, loosen the dirt around each plant with a trowel. Now grab the garlic leaves close to the ground and pull up gently. Be careful that you don't tear the leaves off.

10. Now it's time to braid your garlic. Pick out three bulbs with long leaves and line them up next to each other.

Cut the tops of the leaves so they are all the same length (about 12 inches)

Have a helper hold the bulbs in place while you braid the leaves together.

Tie a ribbon or string around the end of the braid and hang it up in your kitchen.

ROCKY'S GARLIC BRAIDS 2 MILES

Garlic Bread

1 stick of butter

3 cloves of garlic

½ teaspoon italian seasoning

1 loaf of french bread

2 tablespoons grated parmesan cheese

½ teaspoon oregano (from your garden if you have it)

1. Preheat your oven to 350°.

2. Melt the butter in a small saucepan over low heat. As soon as it's all melted, turn the heat off (butter's easy to burn)

3. Peel the dry skin off the garlic, then mash the cloves through a garlic press into the melted butter. Add the herbs and give it all a little stir.

4. Slice the bread lengthwise and brush each half with the butter mixture. Sprinkle the cheese on top.

5. Lay the bread, butter side up on a cookie sheet and bake for 10 minutes.

6. Let the bread cool for a few minutes before you cut it into pieces.

Wiggly Acres Worm Farm

Spring through fall, indoors or outdoors.

Worms aren't as icky as you think. They actually make great garden helpers. They tunnel through the ground under your plants making sure the roots get plenty of air and water. Worms eat dead plants and turn them into a rich food that your plants love. Since a lot of worms make a healthier garden, here's a way to raise some yourself.

You will need:

WIGGLY ACRES
HOME OF HAPPY WORMS
BIRDS KEEP OUT

A large covered container (a cardboard box lined with a garbage bag works well)

Garden soil, potting soil, or compost

A few worms

TOMATOES

COFFEE

Worm food (weeds, leaves, grass clippings, used coffee grounds or fruit and vegetable scraps from your kitchen)

1. Fill the container with soil or compost and mix in 1-2 cups of the worm food. Worms don't like sunshine, so put your container in a cool, shady place. Water the soil so that it is moist, but not soggy.

2. Find some worms. The best place to look is in loose, moist soil. The best time is right after it rains. If worse comes to worse, you can buy some at a fishing store. Red worms are the best.

3. Put your worms in the container. Punch some air holes in the lid, and cover the farm to keep the birds and the rain out. Keep the soil moist and don't forget to give your worms more food now and then. Every few weeks you should stir the soil around to add air to it and to see how many new worms you've grown.

4. After about a month you can start putting your worms to work. Find a few good ones and move them to your garden. Don't worry about covering them with dirt, they'll find their way into the ground. You can also use the soil they've been living in like fertilizer, digging a few handfuls into your garden once a month.

5. Your farm will last a long time if you keep it in the shade, and water and feed the worms regularly.

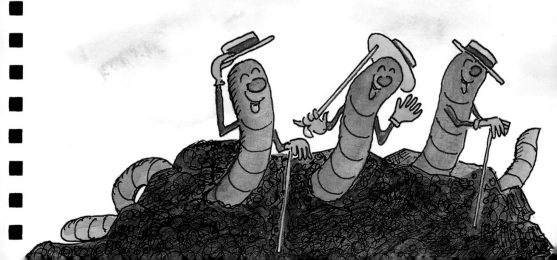

Scarecrow

Having a scarecrow in your garden probably won't scare away too many crows, but they're fun to make and will make your garden feel like a real farm.

Clothes for the scarecrow: a shirt, a pair of pants, gloves, even shoes and a hat if you want

Two sturdy sticks, one about 6 feet long, and another about 4 feet long

An old pillowcase

Heavy string

A permanent marking pen

A few nails

A hammer

Stuffing (straw is best, but dry leaves will work too)

Safety pins

1. Start out by making a frame for your scarecrow. Put the long stick on the ground and lay the short stick across it about 12 inches from the top. Nail the two pieces together (you might need a grown up assistant for this part). Use a couple of nails so that the frame is good and strong.

2. Now pound the frame 12 inches into the ground using the mallet or hammer. If the ground is too hard, soak the spot with lots of water and try the next day. You can always dig a 12 inch deep hole, put your frame in and fill the hole.

3. Use the pillowcase to make a head. Turn it so the open end is down, and draw a face on it. You might want to use a pencil to start, then go over your lines with a permanent marking pen. Fill the pillowcase with straw, then put it over the top of the frame so that the stick goes up into the stuffing. Tie the open end of the pillowcase tightly around the pole with a piece of string.

If you're using a hat, pin it to your scarecrow's head.

4. Tie the ends of the pants closed and fill them with stuffing. Prop them against the frame so that the bottoms are just touching the ground. Tie the pants to the frame by running a piece of string through the back belt loop, then around the stick.

5. The short stick is going to make the scarecrow's arms. Put the shirt on so that the ends of this stick go through the armholes. Tuck the shirt into the pants and button it most of the way up. Fill it with stuffing, tying the arms closed at the cuff when they are full. Button the shirt all the way up, add a little more stuffing, then tuck the ends of the pillowcase into the collar.

6. Fill the gloves with a little stuffing and stick them on the ends of the arms.

7. You can make your scarecrow a little different by tying a bandana around his neck, putting sunglasses on him, or giving him a rake to hold.

Growing activities for young gardeners from Texas to Toronto.

Activities designed for:

- Any place (indoors or out)
- Any season
- Any climate
- Any kid

ISBN 0-932592-25-2   Klutz Press 🍎 Palo Alto, CA